The McGraw-Hill Guide

to
WebCT for Students

How to *Really* Learn Using WebCT

Wes Worsfold

Conestoga College
The Eastbridge Group

Boston   Burr Ridge, IL   Dubuque, IA   Madison, WI   New York   San Francisco   St. Louis
Bangkok   Bogotá   Caracas   Lisbon   London   Madrid
Mexico City   Milan   New Delhi   Seoul   Singapore   Sydney   Taipei   Toronto

Care has been taken to trace ownership of copyright material contained in this text. The publishers will gladly take any information that will enable them to rectify any reference or credit in subsequent editions.

Director of Partnerships and Business Development:	Joe Saundercook
Director: New Media Content Strategies:	Bill Bayer
Production Coordinator:	Melonie Salvati
Supplement Coordinator:	Susan Lombardi
Cover Design:	Craig Jordan
Typeface:	Times New Roman

McGraw-Hill Higher Education

The McGraw-Hill Companies

The McGraw-Hill Guide to WebCT for Students: How to *Really* Learn Using WebCT
Wes Worsfold

The McGraw-Hill Guide to WebCT for Students:
How to *Really* Learn Using WebCT
Wes Worfold

1 2 3 4 5 6 7 8 9 0 FGR/FGR 9 0 9 8 7 6 5 4 3 2 1 0 9

ISBN 0-07-239721-7
     0-07-086100-3 (Canada)

http://www.mhhe.com

ACKNOWLEDGEMENTS

The McGraw-Hill Guide to WebCT for Students was originally conceived and written to serve the students of Conestoga College in Ontario, Canada. We are thankful to all who played a part in the development and production of "WebCT for Students" including the author, Wes Worsfold, Maureen Nummelin from Conestoga College, Joe Saundercook and Kelly Smyth from McGraw-Hill Ryerson, Bill Bayer of McGraw-Hill Higher Education and Suzanne Beaudoin, formerly with McGraw-Hill Ryerson, now with WebCT.

Thanks to WebCT for their cooperation, enthusiasm and expertise in the technical aspects of the review process. We wish to acknowledge in particular the students of Conestoga College for providing constructive criticism and suggestions, and faculty from across the United States and Canada who reviewed the manuscript for accuracy and applicability; all of who were instrumental in the development of the final text. Many thanks to Doug Baleshta, *University College of the Cariboo*, Kevin Barry, *University of Notre Dame,* Norm Friesen, *University of Alberta*, Cable Green, *Ohio State University,* Wayne Ingalls, *University of Maine,* Karen Kier, *Ohio Northern University,* Chet Lyskawa, *University of South Florida,* Wayne Miller, *UCLA,* Bill Moss, *Clemson University,* Anthony Nyman, *Humber College.*

ABOUT THE AUTHOR

Wes Worsfold is an adjunct faculty member with Conestoga College in Kitchener, Ontario, Canada and an Educational Technologies Consultant with The Eastbridge Group. Wes has been using the Internet to deliver educational programs since 1995 and has been using WebCT since it was first released in 1997. Wes has been involved in developing more than 60 online courses and is a frequent presenter on learning technologies. He can be reached at wes@eastbridge-group.com.

ABOUT CONESTOGA COLLEGE

Based in Kitchener, Ontario, Conestoga College serves the growing, dynamic region known as Canada's Technology Triangle for its high concentration of advanced-technology industries and associated business services. The college works in close co-operation with employers to ensure that its programs of study develop appropriately and that graduates are moving into career areas where employment and economic growth exist. Conestoga students prepare for careers in engineering technology and the skilled trades, information technology, business, health sciences, community services and communications.

The college is also active in the expanding fields of postgraduate and adult education programming, international education, and customized training services for business and industry. For more information, contact John Sawicki, Manager, Public Affairs at Jsawicki@conestogac.on.ca

TABLE OF CONTENTS

Foreword.. viii

1   Getting Started with WebCT... 1
    1.1   Equipment Requirements – What do you need?........................... 1
            1.1.1   Your Computer.. 1
            1.1.2   Your Software 2
            1.1.3   Your Browser Settings 3
            1.1.4   Your Internet Access 6
            1.1.5   A Final Word About Software Equipment Requirements 7
    1.2   Accessing Your Course 7
            1.2.1   How do I Login to my Course? 7
            1.2.2   "My WebCT" 8
            1.2.3   How Do I Configure "My WebCT"? 9
            1.2.4   Other Features of the "My WebCT" Page......................... 12
    1.3   Frequently Asked Questions (FAQs) About Using WebCT.................. 19

2   How to Really Use WebCT Course Tools and Features 20
    2.1   Your Course Home Page 20
    2.2   The Course Tools Page.. 21
    2.3   Course Notes Button Bar 21
    2.4   The Navigation Window 22
            2.4.1   How Do I Create a Navigation Window for my Course?......... 23
    2.5   The Course Notes 26
    2.6   Compiling the Course Notes... 27
            2.6.1   How Do I Compile Course Notes?................................ 28
    2.7   Searching Course Notes... 30
            2.7.1   How Do I Search the Course? 30
    2.8   The Glossary... 31
            2.8.1   How Do I Use the Glossary?.................................... 32
    2.9   The Index.. 33
            2.9.1   How Do I Use the Index?....................................... 33
    2.10   Learning Goals and Targets... 34
            2.10.1   How Do I Access Learning Goals and Targets?................... 35
    2.11   Resources and References 36
            2.11.1   How Do I Access Resources and References? 36
    2.12   Image Database 36
            2.12.1   How Do I Use the Image Database?.............................. 37

2.13		Other Multimedia Course Features	38
	2.13.1	How Do I Access Files from the CD?	39
2.14		The Course Outline or Syllabus	40
2.15		Resume Your Last Session	40
2.16		The Course Calendar	40
	2.16.1	How Do I Use the Course Calendar?	41
2.17		The Bulletin Board	42
	2.17.1	How Do I Read Postings from the Bulletin Board?	42
	2.17.2	How Do I Reply to a Posting?	44
	2.17.3	What is a "Thread"?	45
	2.17.4	The Bulletin Board Navigation Bar	45
2.18		The E-mail System	46
	2.18.1	How Do I Read an E-mail Message?	46
	2.18.2	How Do I Write an E-mail Message?	48
	2.18.3	Attaching Files to E-mail Messages and the Bulletin Board	49
	2.18.4	How Do I Attach a File to a Message?	50
	2.18.5	How Do I Download a File?	53
2.19		Chatting Online	55
	2.19.1	How Do I Use the Chat Feature?	55
2.20		Self-Tests	57
	2.20.1	How Do I Complete Self-Tests?	57
2.21		Online Quizzes	59
	2.21.1	How Do I Complete an Online Quiz?	59
	2.21.2	How Do I View My Quiz Marks?	64
2.22		Monitoring Your Progress	66
2.23		Changing Your Password	66
	2.23.1	How Do I Change my Password?	67
2.24		The Assignment Drop Box	68
	2.24.1	How Do I Access an Assignment?	68
	2.24.2	How Do I Submit an Assignment Using the Drop Box?	70
2.25		The White Board	75
	2.25.1	How Do I Use the White Board?	76
2.26		Student Presentations and Home Pages	77
3		More About the Internet and Learning with WebCT	78
3.1		Introduction to the Internet	78
	3.1.1	How did the Internet Start?	78
	3.1.2	What are the Components of the Internet?	79
	3.1.3	How does the Internet Work?	80

3.2   The Browser Window 81
3.3   Searching for Information on the Internet 81
        3.3.1   Search Directories and Search Engines 82
        3.3.2   Tips and Suggestions for Conducting Web Searches 82
3.4   Internet Terminology 83
3.5   Other Resources for Learning about the Internet 84
3.6   The Benefits of Online Learning 85
3.7   Internet Protocols and Etiquette 86
3.8   Communicating Online 87

FOREWORD

Welcome to *The McGraw-Hill Guide to WebCT for Students - How to Really Learn Using WebCT* .

The McGraw-Hill Guide to WebCT for Students - How to Really Learn Using WebCT has been written to provide you with an overview of how to succeed taking a course using WebCT – Web Course Tools. WebCT is a tool that facilitates the creation of sophisticated World Wide Web-based educational environments by non-technical users. We recommend that you thoroughly read *The McGraw-Hill Guide to WebCT for Students - How to Really Learn Using WebCT* before starting your course. *The McGraw-Hill Guide to WebCT for Students - How to Really Learn Using WebCT* will answer most of the questions you may have about taking an online course using WebCT. After reading *The McGraw-Hill Guide to WebCT for Students - How to Really Learn Using WebCT* you will be prepared to start your course.

The McGraw-Hill Guide to WebCT for Students - How to Really Learn Using WebCT is divided into three sections:

Section 1:   **Getting Started with WebCT**
This section provides information about computer and software requirements for using your WebCT course. You'll also learn about how to configure your browser, login to your course and set-up your "my WebCT" page (version 2.0).

Section 2:   **How to Really Use WebCT Course Tools and Features**
This section provides a thorough overview of commonly used WebCT tools and features.

Section 3:   **More About the Internet and Learning with WebCT**
This section provides a brief overview of the Internet and presents some tips and suggestions for making your online learning experience rewarding.

We have endeavoured to make *The McGraw-Hill Guide to WebCT for Students - How to Really Learn Using WebCT* as accurate and as comprehensive as possible. However, changes in technology, software versions and other factors that change over time may affect the accuracy of the manual. We apologize in advance for any discrepancy that you may encounter.
Some of the WebCT features in *The McGraw-Hill Guide to WebCT for Students - How to Really Learn Using WebCT* may only be available to version 2.0 or higher and we have identified these features throughout the book.

Best wishes for success with your course.

Wes Worsfold,
The Eastbridge Group
http://www.eastbridge-group.com
October 1999.

1   GETTING STARTED WITH WEBCT

Technology is revolutionizing the way we work and learn. Computers and the Internet now make it possible to expand the way in which people access information and educational courses.

Online learning does offer many benefits and opportunities to learners. However, online learning also offers challenges and unique considerations for learners. *The McGraw-Hill Guide to WebCT for Students - How to Really Learn Using WebCT* provides you with the foundation to excel in any course that uses WebCT and attempts to address many of the challenges encountered by online learners. This section, Getting Started with WebCT, will help you determine your equipment needs, software requirements and access, and how to set-up your WebCT course.

1.1   Equipment Requirements - What do you need?

The equipment requirements for WebCT courses are relatively simple. For most courses, you will require a computer equipped with Internet software and access to the Internet.

1.1.1   Your Computer

To access online courses you'll need a computer. The brand, make and model does not matter - both Personal Computers (PC-compatibles) and Apple Computers can be used. However, it should be reliable since you need your computer to access your course.

Computer technology changes rapidly, so specifying exact computer requirements may quickly become outdated. However, recommended minimum computer requirements are:

Computer Requirements	
Operating System	A 32-bit operating system is recommended. Some functions in WebCT use software called Java. Java requires 32-bit operating systems to function such as Windows 95/98/NT, O/S 2 Warp and Mac Operating

Computer Requirements	
	System.
Computer Speed	486, Pentium or faster
Computer Memory	Enough computer memory to operate a Web browser (see Software below for more information on Web browsers). At the time of writing, many current Web browsers require 16MB of RAM (Random Access Memory)
Hard Disk Space	Enough disk space to operate a Web browser (see Software below for more information on Web browsers). At the time of writing, many current Web browsers require 50MB of hard drive space.
Modem/Internet Access	A minimum connection speed of 14.4kps or faster (56 kps) is recommended. A fast modem or Internet connection will make accessing your course quicker.

1.1.2 Your Software

The only software requirement for accessing your online course is an Internet browser that can support frames and JavaScript. Two examples of commonly used browsers include Netscape's Navigator and Microsoft's Internet Explorer. Netscape Navigator works best with WebCT and is strongly recommended. Whether you use Netscape's Navigator or Microsoft's Internet Explorer, we recommend you use Version 4 or higher.

You can obtain these browsers free-of-charge by entering one of the Internet addresses below and following the instructions on how to download the software.

Internet Browser Software Downloads	
Browser	**Internet Address**
Netscape Navigator	http://home.netscape.com/download/
Microsoft Internet Explorer	http://www.microsoft.com/

You can also use other Internet browsers, many of which are available free-of-charge over the Internet.

1.1.3 Your Browser Settings

There are two important settings for your browser that you should check before accessing your WebCT course.

1.1.3.1 Java and JavaScript Enabling Your Browser

To use many of the features in your online course such as the self-tests, online quizzes and chat, you need to ensure that your browser is JavaScript and Java enabled.

To enable Java and JavaScript in Netscape 4.x, follow these steps: click on Edit → Preferences → Advanced. Ensure all buttons for Java and JavaScript are enabled as in Figure 1.1.

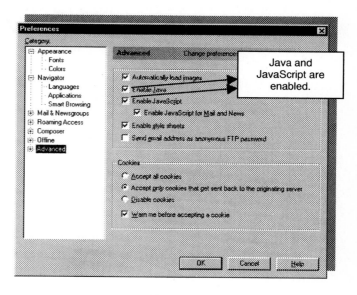

Figure 1.1

To enable Java and JavaScript in Internet Explorer 4.x, follow these steps: Click on View → Internet Options. Click on the Advanced tab and scroll down the screen until you see Java VM. Ensure that the Java JIT compiler and Java logging is enabled by clicking the radio buttons.

For Internet Explorer 5.x, access this from the Tools pull down menu and then click on Internet Options.

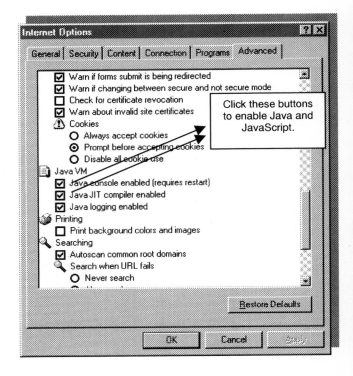

Figure 1.2

1.1.3.2 Cache Settings

Browsers record and save information in a special memory called "cache" when a web site (page) is visited. So, if you happen to visit a web page and then visit the same web page later after changes have been made, your browser may be "calling up" and displaying the saved or "cached" page. Therefore, the page appears with no changes.

For WebCT courses, you should set your browser options so that it does not cache pages. Then, all pages are loaded directly from the server and the most current page is always displayed.

To set the cache settings for Netscape 4.x, follow these steps: click on Edit → Preferences → Advanced → Cache. Ensure the "Every time" button is active under the "Document in cache is compared to document on network" heading.

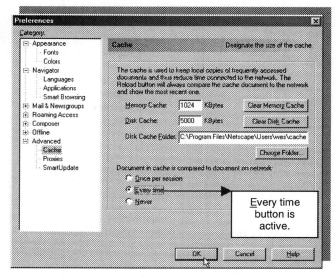

Figure 1. 3

To set the cache settings for Internet Explorer 4.x, follow these steps: Click on View → Internet Options. Click on the General tab and then click the "Settings" button under Temporary Internet files.

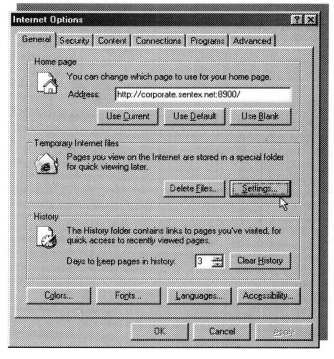

Figure 1. 4

Activate the "Every visit to the page" button.

For Internet Explorer 5.x, access this from the Tools pull down menu and then click on Internet Options.

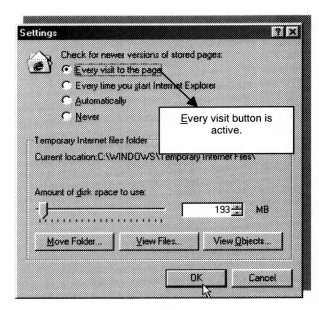

Figure 1. 5

Each browser is different so
review your "Help" instructions on how to configure your browser so that it does not cache pages.

1.1.4 Your Internet Access

Finally, you will need a service to access the Internet. You may be able to access the Internet from your campus. However, if you are going to access your course from home or some place else, you will need an Internet connection.

Companies that provide customers with access to the Internet are called Internet Service Providers (ISPs). For a fee, they allow you to access the Internet from your computer using your modem. ISPs are available in most communities.

1.1.5 A Final Word About Software Equipment Requirements

Some courses may also have additional hardware and software requirements such as a specific word processor, spreadsheet or office suite software. These specific requirements will be identified in the admissions information for your course, or when you first access that course.

1.2 Accessing Your Course

WebCT courses are maintained in a secure environment on the Internet. Only registered students in a course as well as faculty and staff have access to courses.

To access your course you need:

    1. The Internet address (location, or URL) for your course
    2. User Name
    3. Password

You will receive this information from your institution or your instructor.

1.2.1 How do I Login to my Course?

❶ **Locate your course by entering the course address (URL) provided by your instructor or institution in your browser.**

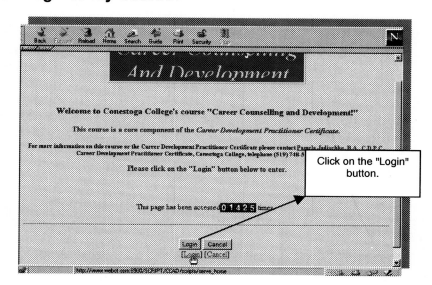

Click on the "Login" button.

Figure 1. 6

Click on the "login" button.

You may also login to your course by locating the WebCT Course Listings page, locating your course name and clicking on it.

❷ **Enter your User Name and Password and then click the "OK" button.**

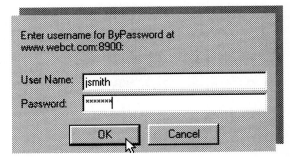

Figure 1.7

❸ **You are now at the home page for your course (Figure 1.8).**

Figure 1.8

1.2.2 "my WebCT"

This is a WebCT Version 2.0 Feature

Depending upon the version of WebCT your institution is using, you may also have the option of customizing

WebCT to suit your own preferences. "my WebCT" allows you to customize your home page and create a single User ID and Password to access multiple WebCT courses. From your "my WebCT" page, you can create your own web links, view announcements and automatically link to new information in your course(s) such as Bulletin Board postings, private e-mail messages, grades, and so on.

1.2.3 How Do I Configure "my WebCT"?

❶ **Click on the <u>Course Listing</u> link from the Course Listing page.**

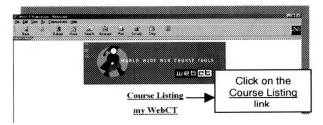

Figure 1. 9

❷ **Click on the course link for the course you want to access.**

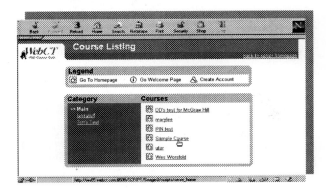

Figure 1.10

❸ **Enter User ID and Password.**

Use the User Name and Password assigned to you by your institution or your instructor.

After entering your User Name and Password, the "my WebCT" SetUp page will open. See figure 1.12.

❹ **If you have never configured your "my WebCT" page, click "No" at the bottom of the page.**

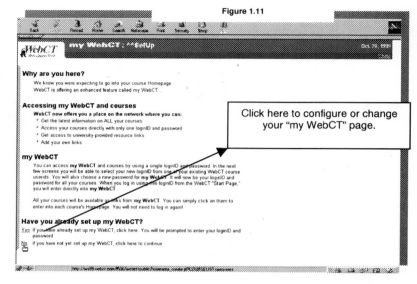

Figure 1.11

Figure 1 .12

❺ **Complete the "Getting Started" section of "my WebCT" by clicking on the "Validate" or "Select" buttons.**

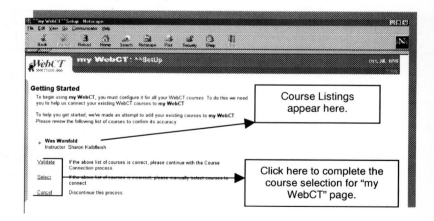

Figure 1. 13

This is where you select your courses for "my WebCT" page.

If you see all the courses you want included in "my WebCT", click on "Validate". Otherwise, click on "Select" to add any other WebCT courses that you are enrolled in.

Once all the courses are listed, click "Validate".

❻ **At the Validate screen, enter the user ID and passwords for each of the WebCT courses you have listed.**

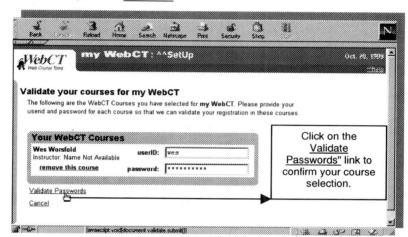

Figure 1. 14

Click on the "Validate Passwords" link to confirm your course selection.

❼ **Set the login ID and Password for your "my WebCT" page by completing the fields required. See figure 1.15. Click the submit link.**

You can select your own login ID and password but it must be one of the existing user IDs for your courses. Once entered, this User Name and Password becomes your new User Name and Password for your "my

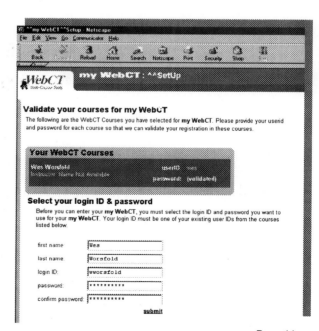

Figure 1. 15

WebCT" page and all your courses.

❽ **Click on the <u>Go to my</u> <u>WebCT</u> link to complete the confirmation process.**

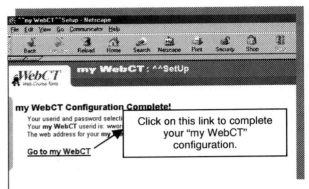

Figure 1. 16

You will be asked to re-enter your new User Name and Password before going to your "my WebCT" page.

Once you have created "my WebCT", all you have to do is choose the "my WebCT" link from the Course Listings page, log on to the "my WebCT" that you have set up, and access all your WebCT courses from that page.

Once you are in your WebCT course, you can return to your "my WebCT" page at any time by clicking the "my WebCT" link that appears on your course Home Page.

1.2.4 Other Features of the "my WebCT" Page

Once your "my WebCT" page has been configured, you have many tools available to customize your page. Some of these tools include:

Add Courses: You can add and delete courses listed on your page.

Access New Items: Any new items such as new private e-mail messages, bulletin board postings, and updated grades for your course(s) appear on your page. Clicking on any of these links will take you directly to the new course information.

Manage Links: Two types of links are available – standard and personal. Your WebCT administrator assigns standard links. However, you can add, delete and re-organize any links that appear under the personal links area.

Information Center: You can also access the WebCT Information Center featuring a variety of educational related information.

Announcements: Your WebCT administrator can add regular announcements that will appear on your "my WebCT" page.

Options: This feature allows you to change your password and merge your "my WebCT" pages.

Help: Online Help is available to guide you through the use of your "my WebCT" page.

Illustrated Features of "my WebCT"

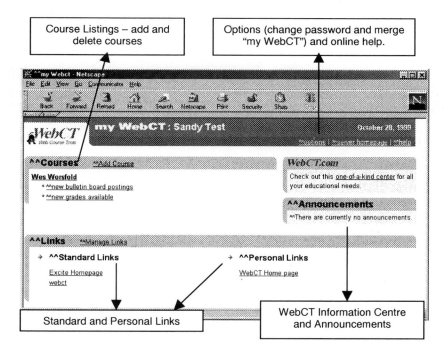

Figure 1. 17

1.3 Frequently Asked Questions (FAQs) About Using WebCT

The following are frequently asked questions that you may have about using the online course system, and their answers.

How do I manage multiple windows when using WebCT courses?

What does this mean? Well, your computer can have many windows open at the same time even though you may only see one window open on your screen. If you fail to close windows through your session, you can have so many windows open that your computer will eventually crash because the systems resources are overburdened.

This frequently occurs when you use a Web browser. When you link to an Internet site or page another window opens. When you are finished visiting the site outside

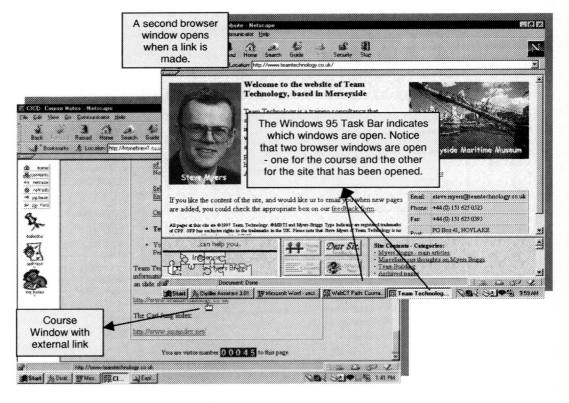

of the course you should close the window to return to the course. You can close the window from the "File" pull down menu and then clicking "Close" (Figure 1.18). You can also close the window using the "close" button on the Window Title Bar.

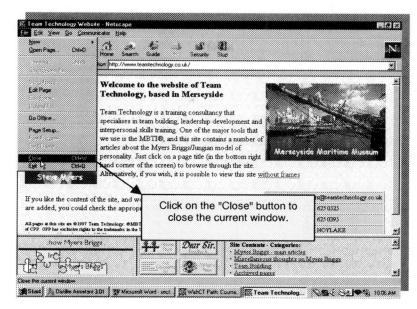

Figure 1 .18

What are cookies? Why do they keep "popping up" as I surf through the course? (Figure 1.19)

Cookies are simple computer files that a Web server sends to your computer so that it knows what parts of an Internet site you are visiting. WebCT courses make extensive use of cookies so that the server knows where you have visited. So, when you click on the "Resume Last Session" button the server knows where you left off. The use of cookies for online courses is harmless.

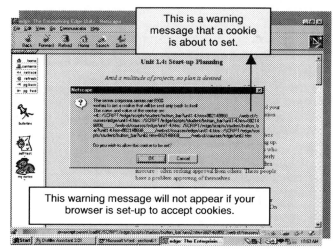

Figure 1. 19

If you find the message that appears on your screen annoying, you can change the setting on your browser to disable the warning. Check your browser help files for instructions on how to disable the cookies warning window. You well never see the cookie warning window if your browser is configured to accept them.

I can't enter the course. What is going on?

There could be a number of reasons why you might not be able to enter the course. Here is a list of some possible causes:

- Are you connected to the Internet? Have you been disconnected? You may be disconnected automatically by your ISP if you have not been active while you are online.

- Do you have the right address (URL) for your course or "my WebCT" page? The address must be absolutely correct to work. You may want to "bookmark" the course address in your browser for future reference ("Bookmarking" is also called "add to favorites" in some browsers).

- Have you entered the correct User ID and Password for the course? Have you used the correct case for each letter (lower and upper case)?

- Is your ISP or computer network firewall stopping you from accessing the course? Some WebCT course addresses or URLs contain a colon (:) followed by a number such as :8900. Some ISPs and computer network firewalls do not allow access to URLs with these types of numbers in them. Consult your ISP technical support, network administrator or Instructor for assistance.

- In very rare circumstances the server that hosts your course may be down for maintenance or repairs or the Internet may be down due to technical problems. Try accessing your course later.

Checking the above may correct your problems.

What are these "Security Information" warnings (Figure 1.20) I receive sometimes especially when I send an e-mail message or post a message to the bulletin board? Is something wrong?

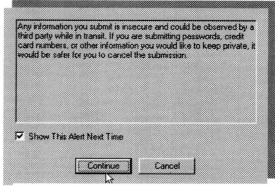

This is a standard message that appears in browsers when you are transmitting (sending) information over the Internet. It is warning you that other people may be able to view, intercept or read what you are sending. The likelihood of anyone intercepting your message is very remote. Simply click "Continue" and send your message.

Figure 1. 20

You can disable this warning message on your browser if you wish. See your browser's Help function for details.

I was in the course but now I can't get back after visiting other sites. Where did it go?

When you visit other sites you may open another browser window. Simply put, you can't return to the course unless you close your active browser window and return to the browser window for your course.

What are JavaScript Errors? (Figure 1.21)

This is a Web server error that originates from the online course software. It cannot harm your computer and in most cases it doesn't affect the function you are performing on the course.

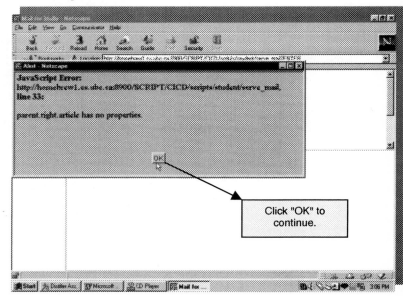

Figure 1. 21

I can't send my e-mail message or bulletin board posting. Why?

If you have composed a very long message, your Internet Service Provider may automatically log you off the Internet.

The solution is to compose your message off line. Simply compose your messages in your word processor and then copy and paste them into the message window.

Can I access the course using AOL's browser?

> We recommend that if you are using America Online for your web access, you use Netscape as the browser instead of AOL's built-in browser. Here's how: connect as usual with AOL, then minimize the window (don't signoff) and open Netscape on your system. Then you can enter the course with Netscape and this should minimize your problems.

Is the course a secure environment?

> Your course environment is a closed, secure environment. Your class is only accessible to registered students, the Instructor, and the administrator. Your instructor may allow visitors, but you should be informed if this occurs.

> Your instructor does have access to the computer log files that advise him/her of your progress in the course - pages visited, time online etc. This is the same information you can view when you access your "Progress" from the course home page.

2 HOW TO REALLY USE WEBCT COURSE TOOLS AND FEATURES

This section provides an overview of the common features you will encounter with WebCT courses. Certainly, each course has its own unique aspects so your course may vary from the examples provided here. Additionally, there are various versions of the WebCT course software so depending upon the version of WebCT used by your Institution you may also encounter some minor differences.

All of the WebCT tools and features described in this section can be accessed from one or more of the following areas of your WebCT course:

- Course Home Page
- Course Tools Page
- Button bar from any path page of course notes
- Navigation Window (WebCT Version 2.0)

2.1 Your Course Home Page

Your Course Home Page links you to the content and features of your course. You can access any of the course features by clicking on any of the icons or links. The specific icons or links for your course will depend upon which tools and features apply to your course.

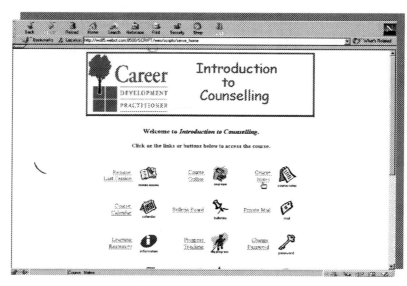

Figure 2.1

2.2 The Course Tools Page

Depending on how your course has been designed, you may also have a Course Tools Page that contains icons and links to WebCT tools and features. Clicking on the icon or link from the Course Home Page accesses the Course Tools Page.

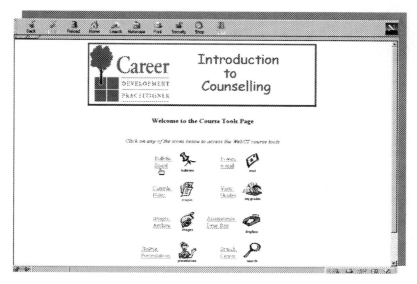

Figure 2.2

2.3 The Course Notes Button Bar

Every path page of your course notes contains a button or navigational bar. This bar appears on the left or top of your browser screen.

See Figure 2.3 for an example of a course button bar.

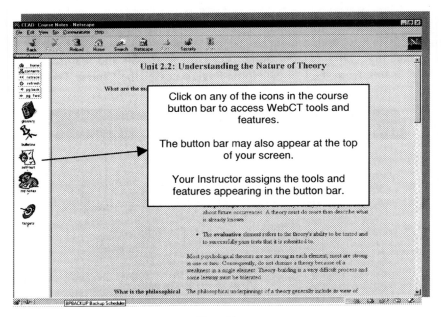

Figure 2.3

2.4 The Navigation Window

The Navigation Window feature of WebCT allows you to create a window containing frequently used icons that stays open as you navigate through the course. This window allows you to access selected WebCT features at any time throughout your course.

This is a WebCT Version 2.0 Feature

See Figure 2.4 for an example of the course Navigation Window.

Figure 2.4

2.4.1 How Do I Create a Navigation Window for my Course?

❶ **Click on the Navigation icon from your Course Home or Tools Page.**

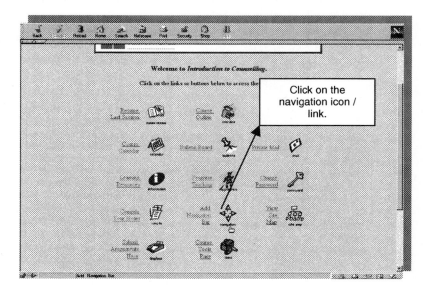

Figure 2.5

❷ Select the Settings button.

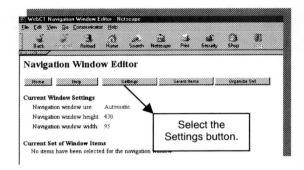

Figure 2.6

❸ Complete the Settings for your Navigation Window.

Choose from the Automatic, Manual, or Off option. Specify the Navigation Window width and height dimensions. Note that the dimensions are measured in pixels.

Click update to save your changes.

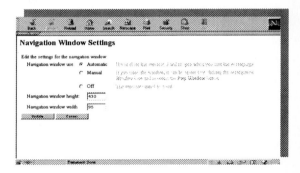

Figure 2.7

❹ **Click the Select Items button. Then, select the WebCT tools you want to appear in the Navigation Window by highlighting the radio buttons beside the features.**

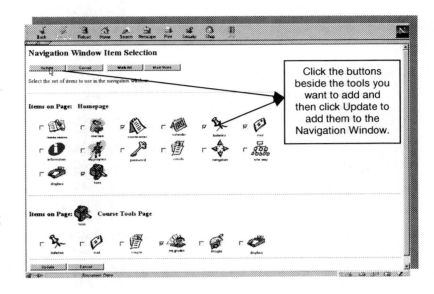

Figure 2.8

Click update to add the tools to your Navigation Window.

The Navigation Window is now accessible at any time during the course (see Figure 2.4).

2.5   The Course Notes

course notes

course notes

Course Notes are path pages created by your instructor to guide you through the course. Each Course Notes appears as a Web page on your screen. You can move through the Course Note pages by using the Page Back and Page Forward icon on the button bar.

❶ **Access the course notes by clicking on the Course Notes icon.**

Course notes contain important information about your course and are created by your instructor.

Click on the "Course Notes" icon / link to access the course notes.

Figure 2.9

Click on any of the Course Notes page links to access that page.

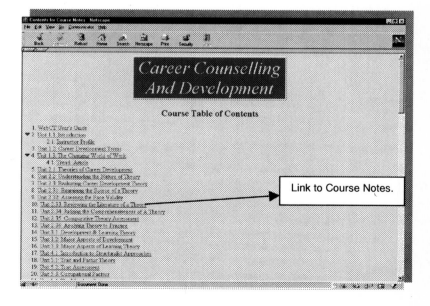

Link to Course Notes.

❸ **Scroll through the course notes or click on the icons in the left frame to access other course features (Figure 2.11).**

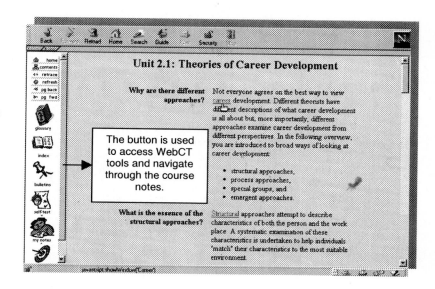

Figure 2.11

2.6 Compiling the Course Notes

You can compile your course notes to create a "mini book" of course pages. This makes it easy to review the course notes. Course notes can also be printed in an easy-to-read straight text format.

2.6.1 How Do I Compile Course Notes?

❶ Click on the Compile button on the Course Home or Tools Page (Figure 2.12).

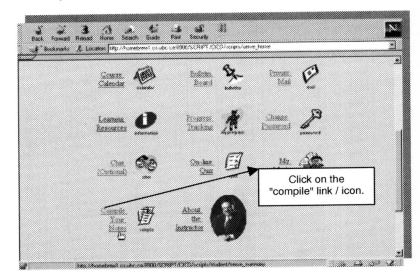

Click on the "compile" link / icon.

Figure 2.12

❷ Select the Course Notes from the Content Compiler.

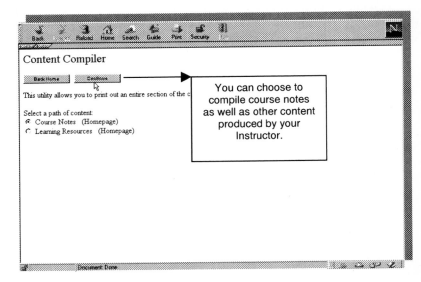

You can choose to compile course notes as well as other content produced by your Instructor.

Figure 2.13

❸ **Select the course notes you want to compile by clicking on the "radio" buttons to the left of the course notes page.**

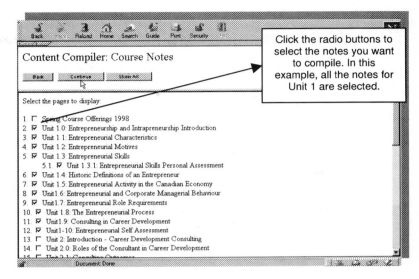

Figure 2.14

❹ **The course notes you have selected to compile now appear on your screen.**

To print the compiled course notes, use the Print Frame command under your browser's File menu.

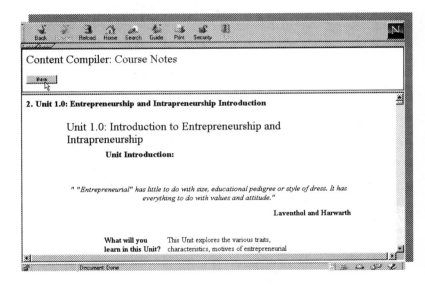

Figure 2.15

overview   search

2.7   Searching Course Notes

You can search your course using the WebCT search tool. This tool allows you to search all text in the course, title, headings, and Bulletin Board postings (version 2.0).

2.7.1 How Do I Search the Course?

❶ **Click on the Search icon on the Course Home or Tools Page (Figure 2.16).**

This opens the "Search the Course" Page (see Figure 2.17).

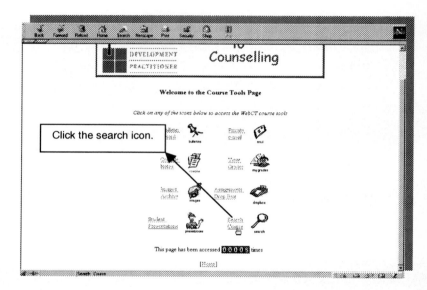

Figure 2.16

❷ **Enter your search scope and the word(s) you are searching. Then, click the Search button.**

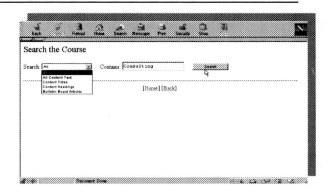

Figure 2.17

❸ **Click on any of the search results links to open the page.**

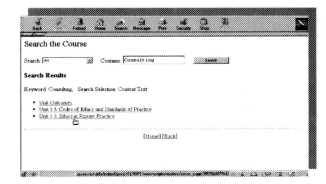

Figure 2.18

2.8   The Glossary

The course glossary provides definitions for words and images in your course assigned by your instructor.

2.8.1 How Do I Use the Glossary?

❶ **Click on the Glossary icon or link on the Course Home or Tools Page (Figure 2.19).**

You may be able to access the Glossary icon or link from the Course Notes Button Bar or Navigation Window.

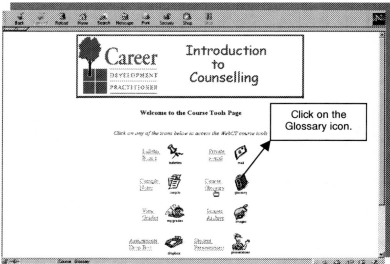

Figure 2.19

❷ **Click on a letter, search, or "view whole glossary" to access the glossary.** *You may also view definitions for specific words that appear as links in your Course.*

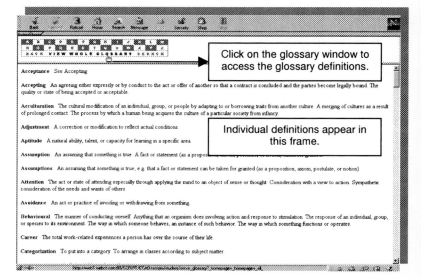

Figure 2.20

2.9 The Index

index

The course index is similar to an index that you find at the back of a textbook. Key words in the course are identified and then added to the index.

2.9.1 How Do I Use the Index?

❶ **Click on the Index icon or link on the Course Home or Tools Page (Figure 2.21).**

You may be able to access the Index icon or link from the Course Notes Button Bar or Navigation Window.

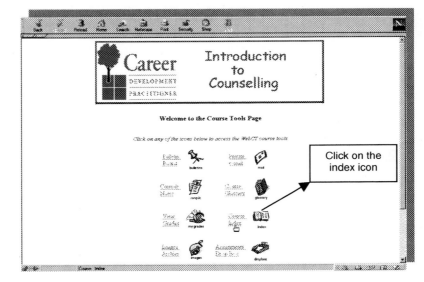

Figure 2. 21

❷ **Click on
any of the
links
appearing
under the
index entry
to access
the page.**

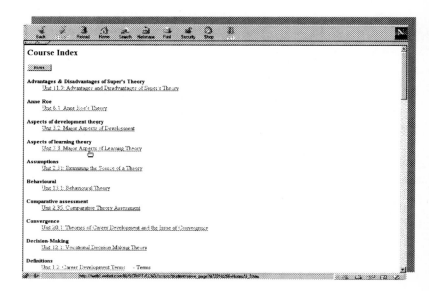

Figure 2.22

2.10 Learning Goals and Targets

targets

Learning goals or targets specify the learning objectives for a Course Notes page.

2.10.1 How Do I Access Learning Goals and Targets?

❶ **Click on the Targets icon or link on the button bar of a Course Notes page (Figure 2.23).**

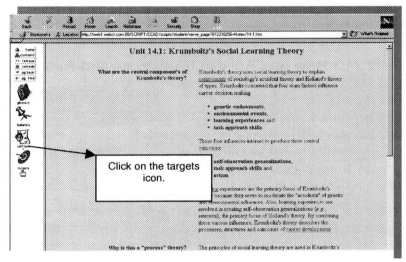

Figure 2. 23

The learning goal or target for the page appears in the Course Notes frame.

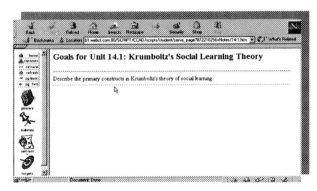

Figure 2. 24

2.11 Resources and References

references

Resources and References contain information about supplementary materials such as articles, books, and Web addresses (URLs).

2.11.1 How do I Access Resources and References?

❶ **Click on the References icon or link on the button bar of a Course Notes page (Figure 2.25).**

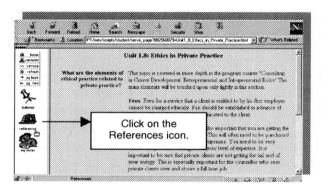

Figure 2. 25

The Resources and References appear in the Course Notes frame.

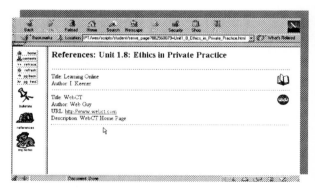

Figure 2. 26

2.12 Image Database

images

The image database allows you to search or browse images, some of which may be entered as thumbnails (a smaller version of the original image).

2.12.1 How do I Use the Image Database?

❶ **Click on the Images icon or link on the Course Home or Tools Page (Figure 2.27).**

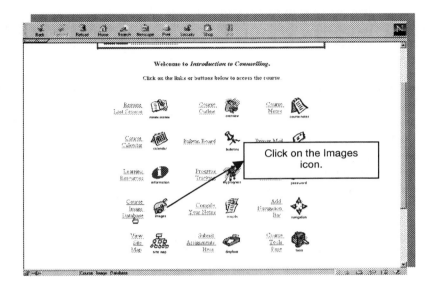

Figure 2. 27

❷ **Click on the link to the image database you want to view.**

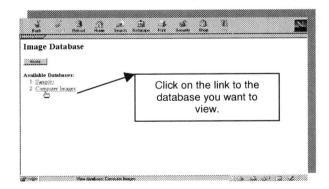

Figure 2. 28

❸ **Click on the "Show All" button to display all the images in the database or use the search feature to locate the image you are seeking.**

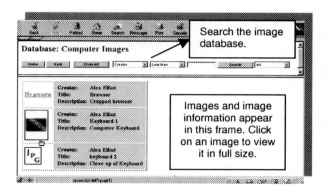

Figure 2. 29

2.13 Other Multimedia Course Features

Courses may contain multimedia features such as video and audio clips. These clips may be downloaded by clicking on the video or audio icon in the button bar of a Course Notes page.

Files for your course may also be added to a CD-ROM that you receive with your course. Specific files can be read from the CD-ROM rather than being downloaded from the Internet. Audio and video files are very large and often take a long time to access on the Internet so accessing them from a CD-ROM saves considerable time (see Figure 2.30).

2.13.1 How Do I Access Files from the CD?

❶ **Click on the CD-ROM icon or link from your Course Home or Tools Page.**

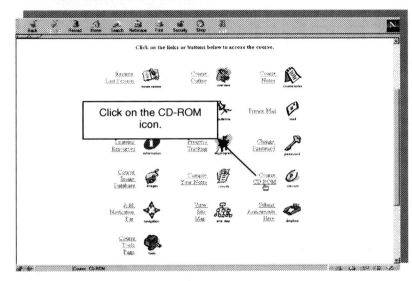

Before using the CD-ROM tools, you must inform WebCT where to find your CD-ROM drive.

Figure 2. 30

❷ **Enter your CD-ROM drive path in the CD-ROM selection window.**

Macintosh users should specify the volume label for the CD-ROM.

Click the Update button to enter your drive path. You'll receive a confirmation that your CD-ROM information has been updated. Click Continue to return to the

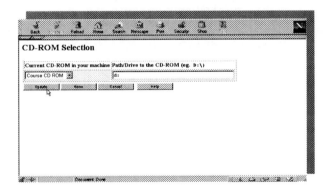

Figure 2. 31

Course Home Page. When you encounter a reference to a multimedia element in a course file, click on the reference's hyperlink to view the element.

2.14 The Course Outline or Syllabus

The course outline or syllabus may be a WebCT path page (similar to Course Notes) or a single page. It specifies the learning objectives, assignments, tests, and marking scheme for the course.

Click on the Course Outline icon on the Course Home Page or Tools Page to access the course outline.

2.15 Resume Your Last Session

You will probably access your course many times and perhaps from different locations---home, work, or the campus. Sometimes it may be difficult to remember where you last left off in the online course.

To begin your online session from where you left off, click on the "Resume Last Session" button from the Home Page. You will be taken automatically to the point in the course where you finished your last session.

2.16 The Course Calendar

The course calendar lists important events and deadlines such as assignment due dates, tests, submission dates for assignments, as well as other relevant course information.

2.16.1 How Do I Use the Course Calendar?

❶ **Click on the Course Calendar icon from the Course Home Page.**

Click on the "Calendar" link / icon.

Figure 2.32

❷ **Click on any of the days of the month to access more information about a posting on the calendar.**

You can also make your own entries to the calendar by clicking on the date link. Your

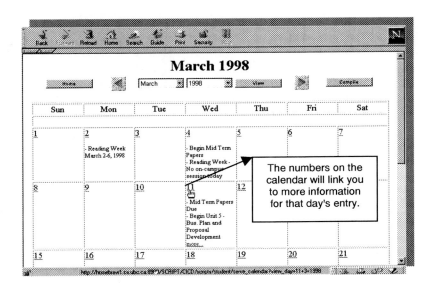

The numbers on the calendar will link you to more information for that day's entry.

Figure 2.33

entries may be private (only you can see them) or public (everyone in the course can see them) depending on the configuration of your course.

2.17 The Bulletin Board

bulletins

bulletins

The Bulletin Board is an important communication tool for students and instructors. It serves as the primary means of group communication for the course.

The Bulletin Board is "public" to anyone registered for the course. Messages can be posted by anyone in the course and can also be read by anyone in the course.

The Bulletin Board is divided into "forums." Every course Bulletin Board has a Main and Notes forum. The Main forum is for general discussions and the Notes forum is for posting from a specific note page of the course. Other forums may exist for your course such as "Hot Sites," "Technical Issues," or "Assignments." Some forums may allow for anonymous postings and some forums may be restricted to certain people in the class, for example, for group projects.

2.17.1 How do I Read Postings from the Bulletin Board?

❶ **Access the Bulletin Board from the Home or Tools Page.**

You may also access the Bulletin Board from the button bar or Navigation Window.

Figure 2.34

You will know when you have unread postings in the Bulletin Board by the icon on the Home Page. When you have unread postings, the icon becomes highlighted like this:

bulletins

❷ **Click on the topic or author's name to read a posting.**

The Bulletin Board is divided into "frames." The left frame contains the navigational buttons. The top frame displays postings.

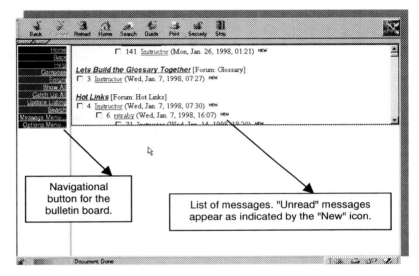

Navigational button for the bulletin board.

List of messages. "Unread" messages appear as indicated by the "New" icon.

Figure 2.35

Click on the "subject" and sender's name to view a message.

The message appears in the bottom frame. You can e-mail a response, reply with another posting, or save the posting.

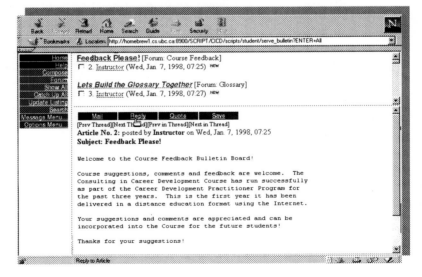

Figure 2.36

2.17.2 How Do I Reply to a Posting?

❶ **Click on the Reply or Quote button.**

Use Reply to respond to the sender's posting.

Use Quote to include a copy of the sender's posting with your response.

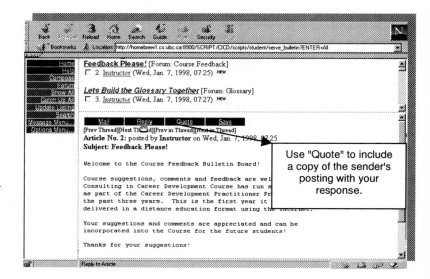

Use "Quote" to include a copy of the sender's posting with your response.

Figure 2.37

❷ **Posting appears as the "next thread" in the list.**

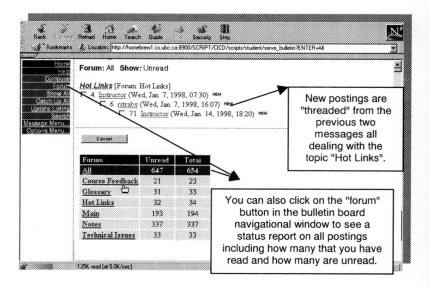

New postings are "threaded" from the previous two messages all dealing with the topic "Hot Links".

You can also click on the "forum" button in the bulletin board navigational window to see a status report on all postings including how many that you have read and how many are unread.

Figure 2.38

2.17.3 What is a "Thread"?

Postings on the bulletin can be "joined" or appear as a "thread." A thread represents a conversation on a given topic. New topics begin a new thread.

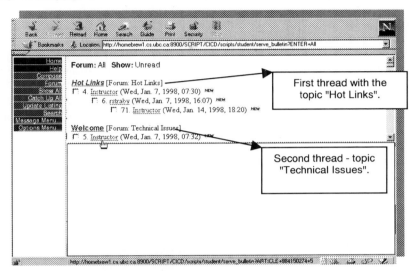

Figure 2.39

2.17.4 The Bulletin Navigation Bar

The Bulletin Board Navigation Bar allows you to access all features of the Bulletin Board.

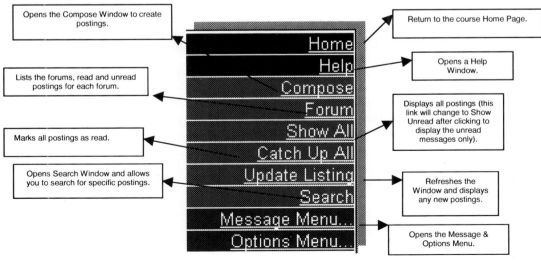

2.18 The E-mail System

The e-mail tool allows you to send a private message to one or more people registered in the course. The structure of the e-mail system is similar in layout to that of the Bulletin Board. Unlike Bulletin Board messages, which are readable by everyone, e-mail is only visible to the sender and receiver(s) of the message. E-mail messages are contained within the course. You cannot send e-mail messages from within the course to people who are not registered in the course.

2.18.1   How do I Read an E-mail Message?

❶ **Click the e-mail icon on the Home Page.**

Figure 2.40

You will know when you have unread e-mail messages by the icon on the home page. When you have unread messages, the icon becomes highlighted like this:

❷ Click the subject or sender's name to read the e-mail message.

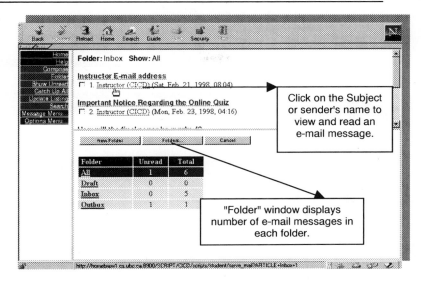

Click on the Subject or sender's name to view and read an e-mail message.

"Folder" window displays number of e-mail messages in each folder.

Figure 2.41

Read the message and reply using the Reply or Quote button.

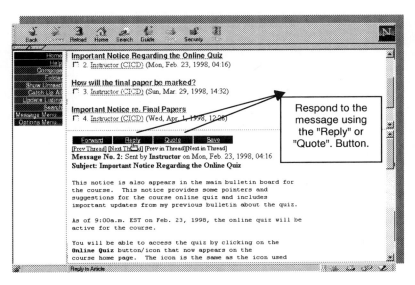

Respond to the message using the "Reply" or "Quote". Button.

Figure 2.42

2.18.2 How Do I Write an E-mail Message?

❶ **Click the e-mail icon on the Home or Tools Page (see Figure 2.40).**

Click on the Compose button and enter the e-mail compose window.

To view a list of people to send

messages to, click the Browse button.

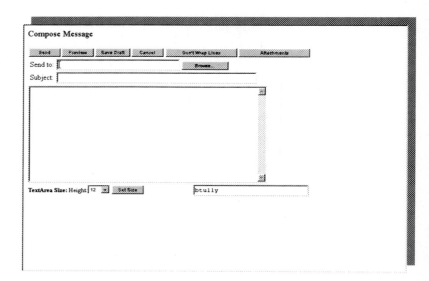

Figure 2.43

❷ **Select to whom you want to send a message.**

Click and highlight the names you want to send your message to and then click OK.

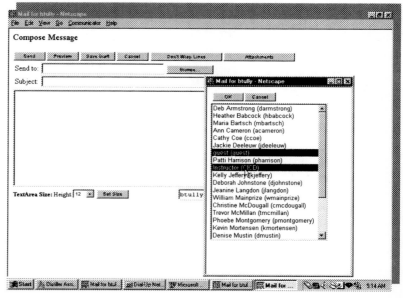

Figure 2.44

If you want to select names that are not adjacent, hold down the CTRL key as you click on each name.

❸ **Complete the Subject and Message in the Windows provided and click Send to send your message.**

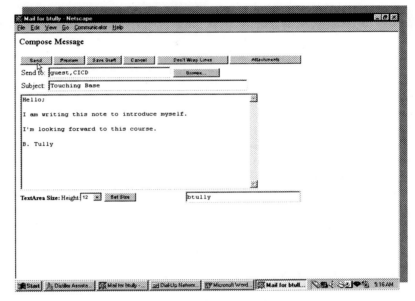

Figure 2.45

2.18.3 Attaching Files to E-mail Messages and the Bulletin Board

The Bulletin Board and the e-mail tools both have an "Attachment" button that allows you to "attach" files to your e-mail message without any laborious copying and pasting. The process outlined below is the same for both the private e-mail system and the Bulletin Board.

2.18.4 How Do I Attach a File to a Message?

❶ Click the Compose button to create a new message.

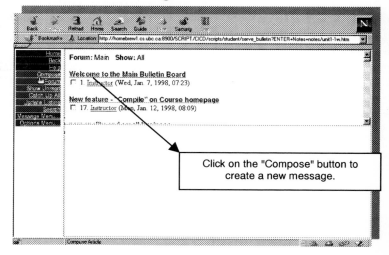

Click on the "Compose" button to create a new message.

Figure 2.46

❷ Enter the subject line and other information as usual.

Key in your message into the message window. It's usually a good idea to explain to the recipient what to expect in the attachment.

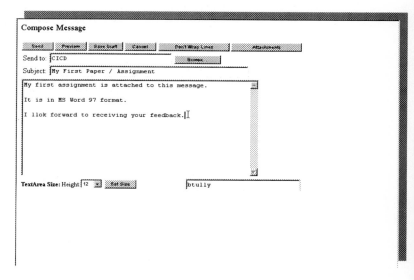

Figure 2.47

❸ **Click on the Attach button.**

A new window will come up, asking for file information.

The Attach Window will appear. Click on the Attach button at the top of that window.

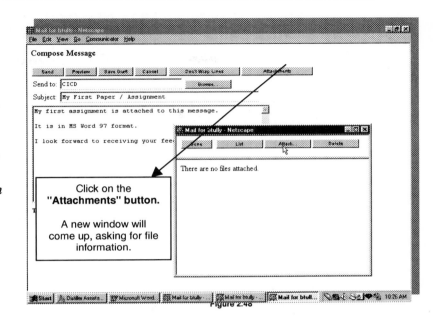

Figure 2.48

❸ **When Browse appears in the lower part of the Attach window, enter the path and the name of the file on your computer or click the Browse button.**

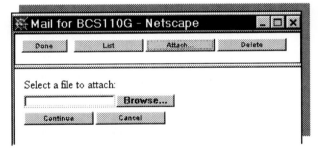

Figure 2.49

❹ **At the File Upload window, locate the file on your hard drive or disk that you want to send along. Once you find the directory on your computer, if you do not see your file listed, be sure that the "Files of Type" window shows All Files.**

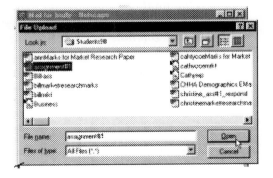

Once you find the file, double click on it.

Its name and path will appear in the Browse window on the Attach screen. Click on Continue.

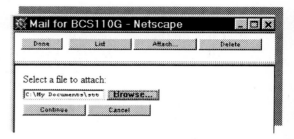

Figure 2.50

The Attach screen will now show the file name and size. Be sure that the file size is not 0. A file size of 0 means that the attachment was not successful and you need to repeat the process.

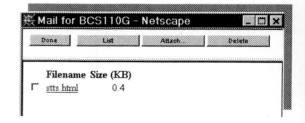

Figure 2.51

❺ **Then click on the Done button, and you'll be back to your main message window.**

Finish your message, click on the Send button, and your message will go along with the attachment.

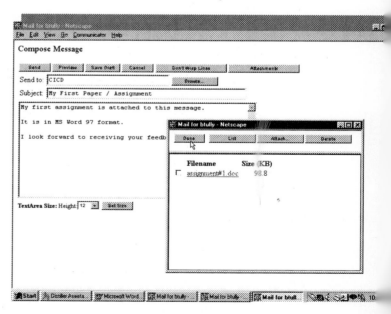

Figure 2.52

You can check to see if your file is attached by clicking the Preview button before sending the message. The Attachment button will appear in your message. See Figure 2.53.

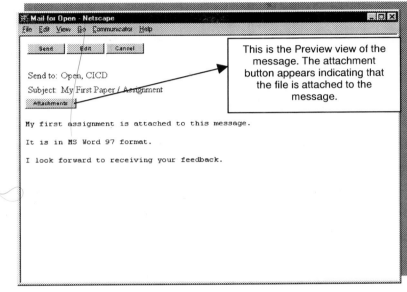

Figure 2.53

2.18.5 How Do I Download a File?

To download a file that is attached to a message, click on the Attachment button in the message body.

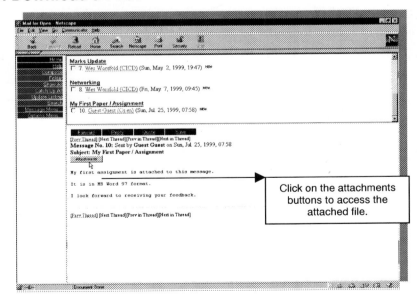

Figure 2.54

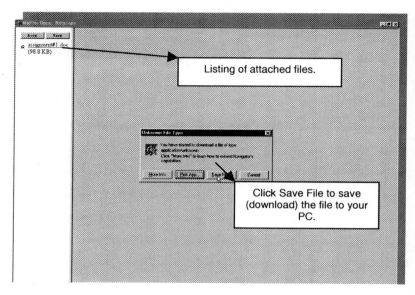

Another window will open and you will be prompted to save the file.

Listing of attached files.

Click Save File to save (download) the file to your PC.

Figure 2.55

Indicate the folder and file name for saving (downloading) the file to your PC.

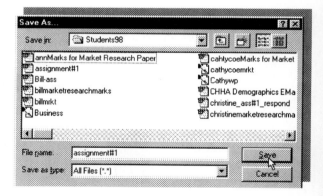

Figure 2.56

The file will be saved
(downloaded) to your
computer.

You will now be able to open
the file from your computer
using the appropriate
software.

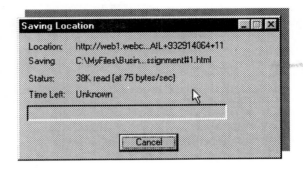

Figure 2.57

2.19 Chatting Online

The chat feature allows you to have "real-time" conversations with other people
registered in the course. This feature is useful if you want to have a "meeting" with
another student. You may want to arrange the time for your chat session ahead of
time using the Bulletin Board or e-mail system.

2.19.1 How Do I Use the Chat Feature?

❶ Click on
the Chat
icon on the
Course
Home
Page.

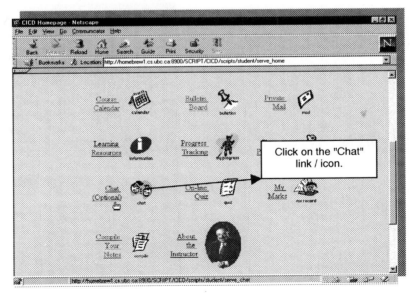

Figure 2.58

❷ **Click on the "room" you want to enter.**

There are four general-purpose chat "rooms" and one general forum for the course and one for all courses. These rooms are areas to hold your conversations. To enter a room, simply click on it once. (If you double click, you will be shown as being in the chat room twice!)

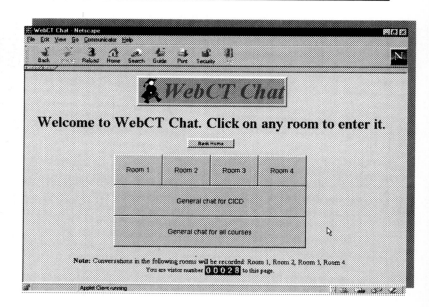

Figure 2.59

Enter a message.

Enter a message in the message window.

There may be a delay before your message appears in the output box.

Click on Quit to exit and finish your session.

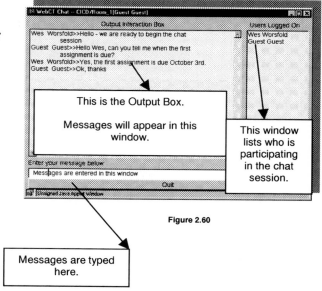

Figure 2.60

This is the Output Box.

Messages will appear in this window.

This window lists who is participating in the chat session.

Messages are typed here.

2.20 Self-Tests

Self-Tests are automated Multiple Choice and True and False tests that you complete to review course materials and test your knowledge. The Self-Tests are not marked or graded and you can complete them anytime and as many times as you want.

2.20.1 How Do I Complete Self-Tests?

❶ **Click on the Self-Test icon in the course notes button bar.**

Self-Tests may also be accessed from the Home or Tools Page.

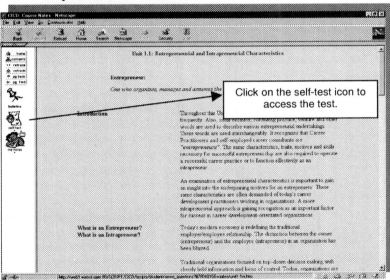

Click on the self-test icon to access the test.

Figure 2.61

❷ **The Self-Test will open in the course notes frame.**

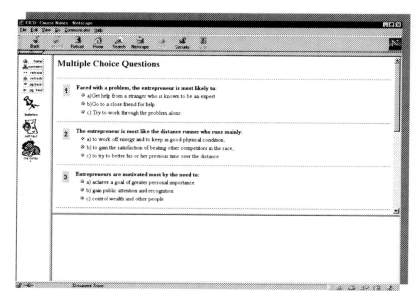

Figure 2.62

❸ **Click on the answer to the question.**

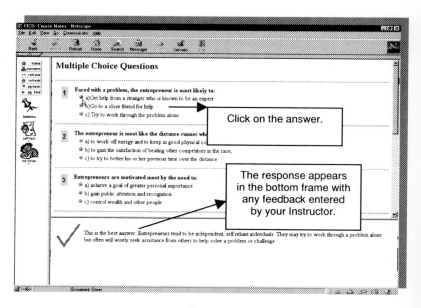

Figure 2.63

2.21 Online Quizzes

Online quizzes are automated tests that are marked by the course software. Quizzes can take a variety of forms including True and False, Multiple Choice, Matching, and Short Answer.

2.21.1 How Do I Complete an Online Quiz?

❶ **Click on the Quiz from the Course Home Page.**

The Quiz icon may also appear in the button bar of a course note page.

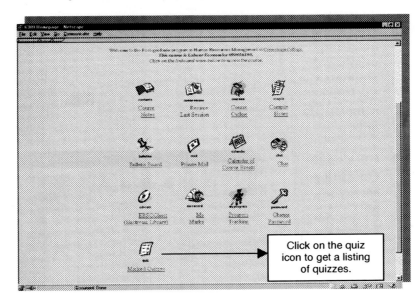

Click on the quiz icon to get a listing of quizzes.

Figure 2.64

❷ The list of all quizzes for the course appears as well as information about when the quiz is available, the duration or time of the quiz, and number of attempts you have to complete the quiz.

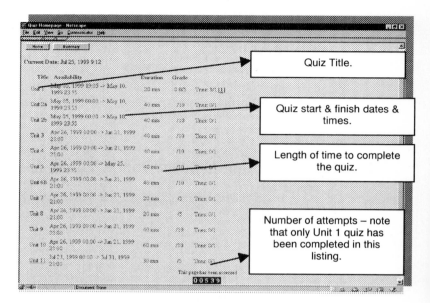

Quiz Title.

Quiz start & finish dates & times.

Length of time to complete the quiz.

Number of attempts – note that only Unit 1 quiz has been completed in this listing.

Figure 2.65

❸ Click on the Quiz title to enter the quiz.

Before entering the quiz ensure you have prepared for the test and know the material that is going to be covered and the length of time you have to complete the quiz.

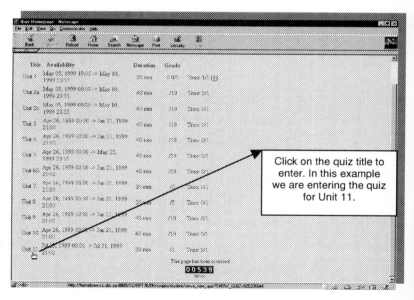

Click on the quiz title to enter. In this example we are entering the quiz for Unit 11.

Figure 2.66

❹ **Upon entering the quiz, you'll be notified about how much time you have to complete it.**

Once you have entered the quiz, "the clock starts ticking" and you must complete the quiz.

This is the actual quiz screen.

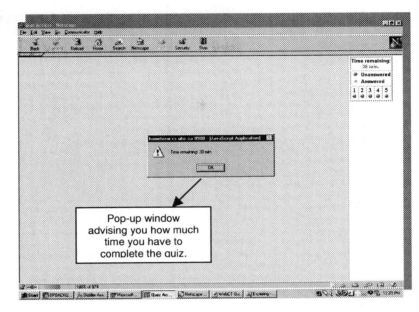

Pop-up window advising you how much time you have to complete the quiz.

Figure 2.67

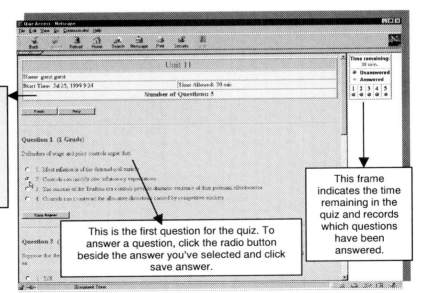

This part of the quiz provides you with information about the quiz such as your start date and time, time allowed for completion, and number of questions.

This is the first question for the quiz. To answer a question, click the radio button beside the answer you've selected and click save answer.

This frame indicates the time remaining in the quiz and records which questions have been answered.

Figure 2.68

❺ **After saving your answers for each question, click the Finish button to submit the quiz for marking.**

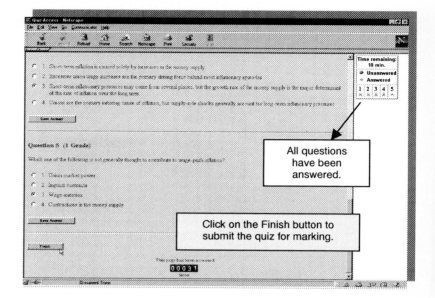

All questions have been answered.

Click on the Finish button to submit the quiz for marking.

Figure 2.69

After clicking the Finish button, you'll receive a reminder confirming that you want the quiz to be submitted for marking.

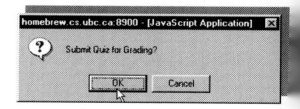

Figure 2.70

After submitting the quiz you'll receive notification that the quiz has been submitted and you can return to the Course Home Page.

If there is a View Results button on this screen, you can click on it and immediately go into your quiz to see how you did.

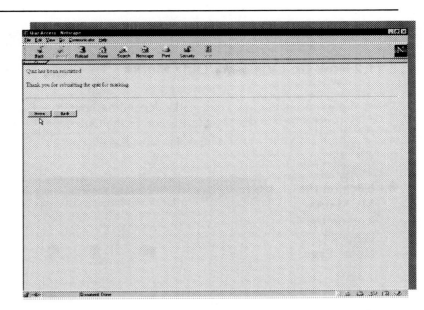

Figure 2.71

2.21.2 How Do I View My Quiz Marks?

There are two ways to view your marks depending upon how your instructor has configured the course---the My Marks icon or the Quiz icon. Please note that the configuration for your course may vary. Check with your instructor for the specifics of your course.

❶ **Click on the My Marks icon on the Course Home Page.**

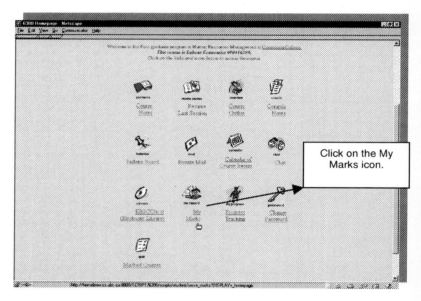

Figure 2.72

Provided your instructor has released your quiz scores, you will be able to see your grade.

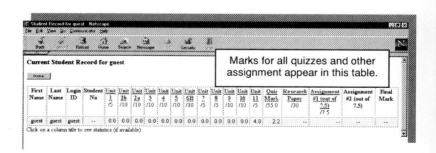

Figure 2. 73

❷ **Click on the quiz icon on the Course Home Page and the list of all quizzes will appear.**

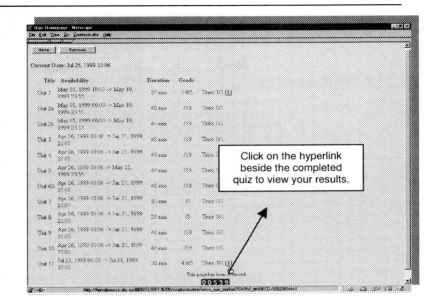

Click on the hyperlink beside the completed quiz to view your results.

Figure 2.74

Depending upon how your instructor has configured your course, you will be able to view varying degrees of details about your performance. Your course may vary from this example.

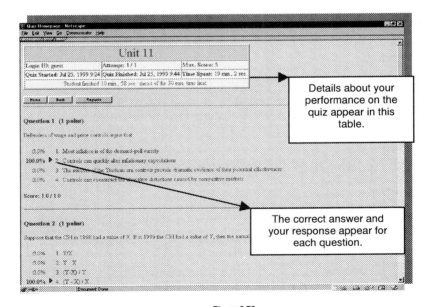

Details about your performance on the quiz appear in this table.

The correct answer and your response appear for each question.

Figure 2.75

2.22 Monitoring Your Progress

The "my progress" feature shows progress about your use of the course. Information and graphs about which portions of the course were accessed, how many, what percentages of the pages in the course

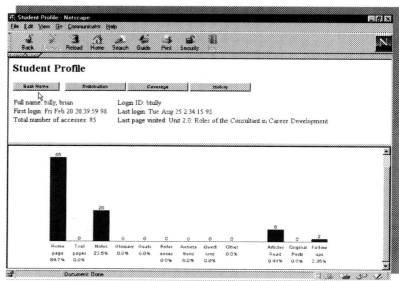

Figure 2.76

were accessed, and the histories of pages visited are displayed.

An example is shown in Figure 2.76. The information you can access from the "my progress" icon is also available to your instructor.

2.23 Changing Your Password

Access to your course is protected by your password. No one else has access to your password but you! Your password should be treated with the strictest of confidence and should not be shared with anyone else.

You may want to change your password periodically as a security precaution.

2.23.1 How Do I Change My Password?

❶ Click on the Change Password icon from the Home or Tools Page.

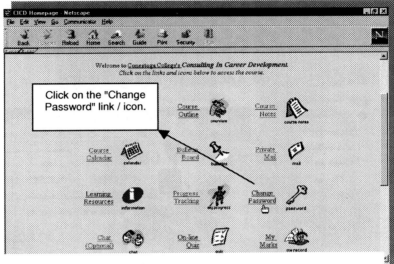

Figure 2.77

❷ Enter the new Password in both text boxes.

You will then have to enter the new Password before you can continue in the course.

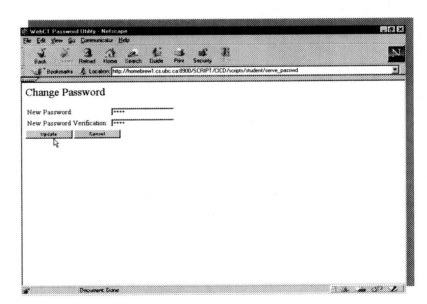

Figure 2.78

2.24 The Assignment Drop Box

dropbox

The Assignment Drop Box tool allows you to receive an assignment from your instructor. It also allows you to submit completed assignments to your instructor or marker.

This is a WebCT Version 2.0 Feature

2.24.1 How Do I Access an Assignment?

❶ Access the Assignment Drop Box by clicking on the icon / link from your Course Home or Tools Page.

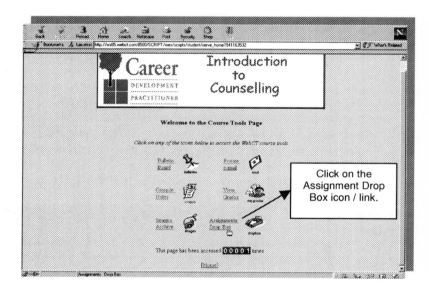

Click on the Assignment Drop Box icon / link.

Figure 2.79

❷ **Click on the Assignment link to access the assignment you want to access.**

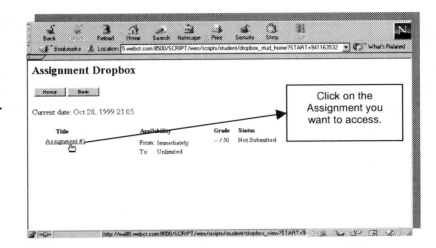

Figure 2.80

❸ **Click on the Files link to view or download any file(s) from your instructor related to the Assignment.**

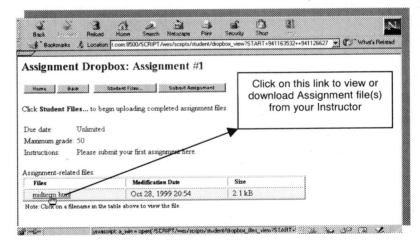

Figure 2.81

Another Window opens displaying the file(s) and provides you with the option of downloading the file to your computer.

Click on the Done button to close the Window.

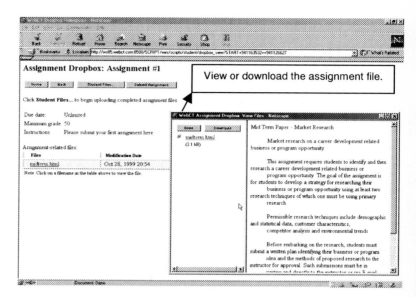

Figure 2.82

2.24.2 How Do I Submit an Assignment Using the Drop Box?

❶ **Access the Assignment Drop Box by clicking on the icon/link from your Home or Tools Page.**

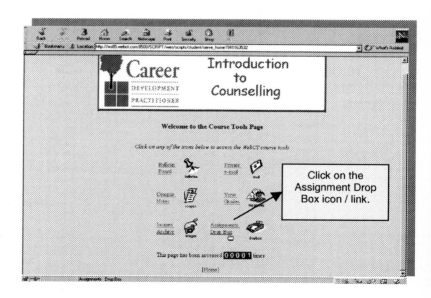

Figure 2.83

❷ **Click on the Assignment link to access your assignment.**

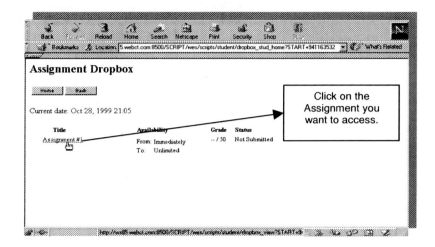

Figure 2.84

❸ **Click on the Student Files button.**

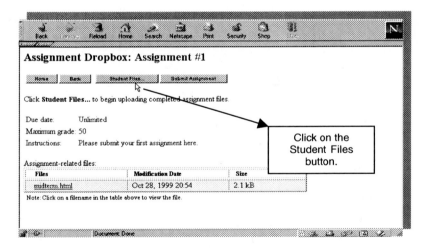

Figure 2.85

❹ **Click on the Upload button.**

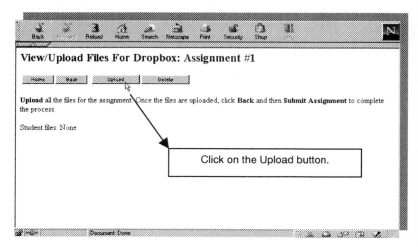

View/Upload Files For Dropbox: Assignment #1

Upload all the files for the assignment. Once the files are uploaded, click **Back** and then **Submit Assignment** to complete the process.

Student files: None

Click on the Upload button.

Figure 2.86

❺ **Enter the path in the Filename window or click Browse to locate your file.**

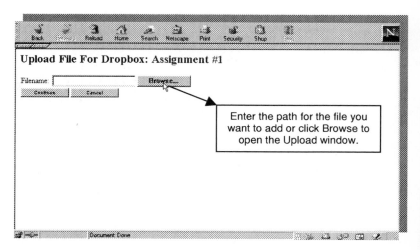

Upload File For Dropbox: Assignment #1

Filename: Browse...

Enter the path for the file you want to add or click Browse to open the Upload window.

Figure 2.87

❻ **Enter the path and filename or locate the file you want to upload on your local computer. Highlight the file and click Open.**

The file will appear in the Upload window. Click Continue to upload the file.

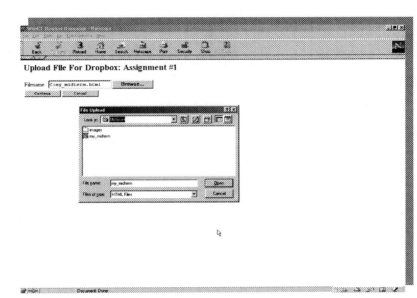

Figure 2.88

❼ **Once the file(s) is uploaded, click Back and then Submit Assignment to complete the process.**

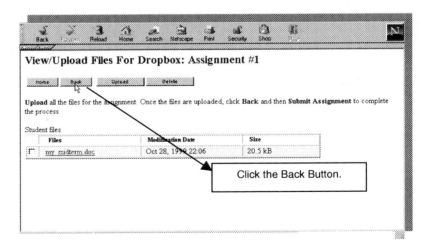

Figure 2.89

Click the Submit Assignment button.

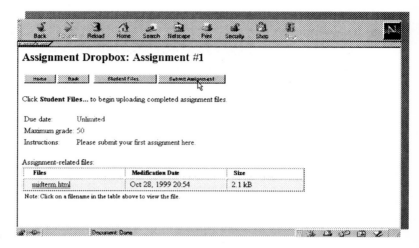

Figure 2.90

Click the OK button to submit the Assignment.

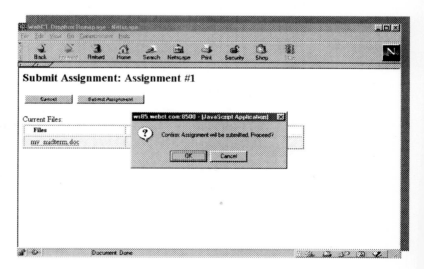

Figure 2.91

You'll return to the Assignment Drop Box window after submitting your assignment.

Assignment Dropbox

Home | Back

Current date: Oct 28, 1999 22:13

Title	Availability	Grade	Status
Assignment #1	From: Immediately To: Unlimited	-- / 50	Not Graded

Click the Home button to return to the Course Home Page.

Figure 2.92

Please note that once you have submitted your assignment, you do not have an opportunity to re-submit the assignment unless the instructor resets your Assignment Drop Box.

2.25 The White Board

white board

The White Board allows groups of students and instructors to use graphical images in "real time." The White Board offers drawing tools, including the ability to insert text and graphics, choose fonts and colours, fill and un-fill objects, move objects, and modify them. This is a useful tool for online group discussions where diagrams are needed.

2.25.1 How Do I Use the White Board?

❶ Click on the White Board icon or link from the Course Home or Tools Page.

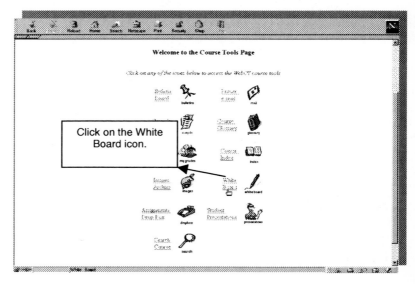

Figure 2.93

❷ Click the Start White Board button once to open the White Board.

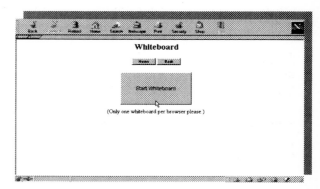

Figure 2.94

Use the controls at the side and bottom of the White Board to create text and images in the White Board space. To close the White Board, click File → Close.

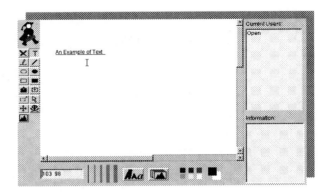

Figure 2.95

2.26 Student Presentations and Home Pages

Two other WebCT course features include Student Presentations and Student Home Pages.

Student presentations allow you to add a multimedia presentation to the course for others to view. The presentation must be created in Hypertext Markup Language (HTML) so some knowledge of HTML is required.

Student Home Pages allows you to create a Home Page about yourself for others in the course to view. Home pages are created using clickable buttons built into WebCT.

Both Student Presentations and Home Pages may be accessed from the Course Home or Tools Page. Instructions are visible on each screen to guide you through the process of creating Presentation and Home Pages.

3 MORE ABOUT THE INTERNET AND LEARNING WITH WEBCT

This section provides you with general information about the Internet and suggestions for using WebCT effectively to make the most of your online learning experience.

3.1 Introduction to the Internet

You have no doubt heard of the Internet. You can't open a newspaper, listen to the radio, or watch television without being exposed to the information explosion. The Internet is changing the way we receive information, work and learn. Despite its popularity, many people don't know how the Internet started or how it functions.

3.1.1 How did the Internet Start?

The Internet (also commonly referred to as "the Net") has existed since the 1960s. In 1969, the US Department of Defence linked four computers at Stanford Research Institute, University of California at Los Angeles, the University of Utah and the University of California-Santa Barbara. This created a "network" of computers that could transfer information regarding government projects of interest to the researchers. Although the network grew during the 1970s, the expense of computers and complexity of computer interfaces resulted in no more than a few thousand people using the network.

It wasn't until personal computers lowered in price and gained acceptance in people's homes that the potential of the Internet became known. Tim Berners-Lee further boosted the acceptance of the Internet while working at the high-energy physics laboratory in Geneva, CERN. Tim Berners-Lee envisioned taking the Internet to its next level by making information accessible through any computer on a network. The Internet provided this vehicle.

With the release of Mosaic in 1993, a graphical, Windows-type interface, information could now be retrieved easily on any computer and by most users. Other Windows-type browsers became available. Internet Service Providers, companies that allow clients to call a phone number via modem and log onto the Net made connecting to the Internet accessible to anyone with a personal computer, phone line and modem. Today, an estimated 150 million people use the Internet and the number is growing rapidly. The computers that comprise the network, or servers, continue to grow to allow more information and accessibility.

3.1.2   What are the Components of the Internet?

Most people think of the Internet as a system that lets you send and receive e-mail messages and "surf" for information. In reality, the Internet provides a host of activities and services. Some of these activities and services include:

- **Electronic Mail (e-mail):** E-mail services allow you to send and receive messages to anyone else having an e-mail address and e-mail service. You can attach computer files to e-mail messages containing information, computer programs, pictures, sounds and any form of information that can be converted to a digitized computer format. E-mail is the most frequently used service of the Internet.

-

- **World Wide Web (WWW):** Also known as the Web, the World Wide Web is a collection of documents on the Internet linked together by a "hypermedia system". This allows users to "Point and Click" on "hyperlinks" to access text, graphics, video, or audio. To access information on the Web, you need an Web browser such as Netscape's Navigator or Microsoft's Internet Explorer to view documents.

-

- **Telnet**: Allows you to log onto another remote computer and to work with that computer in much the same way you would if you were directly connected to it.

-

- **File Transfer Protocol (FTP):** FTP is a high-speed means of transferring computer files between computers on the Internet. It is useful for uploading and downloading information to and from the Internet.

There are many other components to the Internet. For WebCT courses, you will only require access to the World Wide Web. E-mail communications between students and the instructor for your course are available within the course.

3.1.3 How does the Internet Work?

Your computer connects to the Internet through its modem to an Internet Service Provider (ISP) who in turn connects you to the Internet and the World Wide Web.

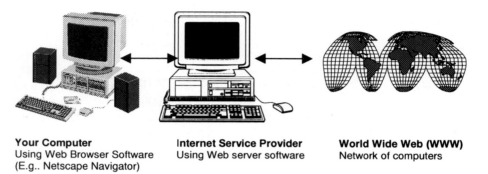

Your Computer
Using Web Browser Software
(E.g.. Netscape Navigator)

Internet Service Provider
Using Web server software

World Wide Web (WWW)
Network of computers

First, you make a request for information from the Internet (i.e. type an http:// address or click a *hyperlink)*. Then the Internet sends back information to you and it is displayed by your Browser (e.g. Netscape Navigator).

3.2   The Browser Window

A Web page may contain text and multimedia (images, movies, and sound). The location of an Internet page or site is called an Internet address or the URL (Universal Resource Locator).

The Netscape Home Page is displayed below in the Netscape Navigator browser:

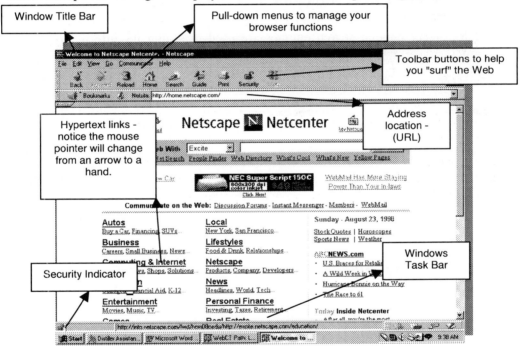

3.3   Searching for Information on the Internet

A recent ad for a computer company stated: *"What's good about the Internet is the amount of information. What's bad about the Internet is the amount of information!"*

To find the information you want, it helps to know how to conduct searches on the Internet.

Fortunately, to help you find what you want, there are a number of great tools on the Internet called "search directories" and "search engines". Becoming proficient in using these tools will make it easier and quicker the information and resources you want.

3.3.1 Search Directories and Search Engines

The following popular search engines are used to search for information on the Internet.

Search Directories and Search Engines	
Search Directory/Engine	**Internet Address (URL)**
Yahoo	http://www.yahoo.com or http://www.yahoo.ca
Excite	http://www.excite.com
Infoseek	http://infoseek.go.com/
AltaVista	http://altavista.digital.com
WebCrawler	http://webcrawler.com/
Lycos	http://www.lycos.com/

3.3.2 Tips and Suggestions for Conducting Web Searches

You may find these tips and suggestions useful when searching for resources:

1. Since each search engine collects and organizes information in different ways, it maybe a good idea to use more than one search engine to find the information you want.

2. Many search engines provide an index of information. You may want to start by searching one of the indices for the information you require. For example, Yahoo includes predefined categories of information.

3. Most search engines organize information based upon "keywords". Start by identifying the "keywords" that apply to your search. Often it

is helpful to "narrow" your search by being as specific as possible with your keywords.

4. Use more than one keyword in your searches. Most search engines allow you to create a "string" of keywords and use "boolean" operators (such as boolean **or**; boolean **and**). Examples of boolean searches include: "WebCT college **and** learning"; "WebCT **or** learning".

5. You may also use features of the search engine itself to aid in your quest for information. Some search tools feature advanced search options or features to search Web page titles or entire Web page contents for results.

3.4   Internet Terminology

Internet Terminology	
Internet	An international network connecting approximately 36,000 smaller networks that links computers at academic, scientific, and commercial institutions. It is accessible to anyone with a computer, a modem, and an Internet Service Provider (ISP).
Information Superhighway	A euphemism for the Internet. The Information Superhighway is envisioned as fundamentally changing the nature of communications and hence society, business, governments, and personal life.
Electronic Mail (e-mail)	A method of composing, editing, sending, and receiving messages (mail) electronically.
Telnet	Provides capability to login to a remote computer and work interactively with it. Running a Telnet session remotely connects your computer to a computer at a different location, but it acts as if you are directly connected to that computer.

File Transfer Protocol (FTP)	A method that allows you to move files and data from one computer to another. FTP allows you to download magazines, books, documents, free software, music, graphics and more.
Browser (Web Browser)	Software that enables people to view Web sites on their computers. Without browser software, users cannot use the part of the Internet called the World Wide Web. Two of the most common browsers are Netscape Navigator and Microsoft Internet Explorer.
Hypermedia System (Links)	The Web is a collection of documents linked together in a hypermedia system. Links can point to any location on the Internet that can contain information in the form of text, graphics, video or sound files.
Universal Resource Locators (URLs)	A standard format for identifying locations on the Web. They allow an addressing system for other Internet protocols such as access to Gopher menus, FTP file retrieval, and Usenet newsgroups.
Hypertext Markup Language (HTML)	A set of instructions, called tags or markups, that are used for documents on the Web to specify document structure, formatting, and links to other documents.

3.5   Other Resources for Learning about the Internet

If you are interested in learning more about the Internet and how to use it effectively, there are many books and magazines that deal with the Internet - just check your local library or bookstore.

There are also many resources online. Countless Web sites have plenty of information about how to use the Internet. One of the most comprehensive sites is the University of Berkeley's Internet Guide. It contains information on how to use the Internet and detailed information on conducting effective searches. You can find the site at:
http://www.lib.berkeley.edu/TeachingLib/Guides/Internet/FindInfo.html

3.6   The Benefits of Online Learning

WebCT courses make it possible for students to access courses and programs in a more flexible way than is available through traditional classrooms, presentations and lectures.

Some of benefits of learning with WebCT courses include:

- **More flexibility**: Online courses allow you to access your course at a time that best suits your personal schedule. However, all courses have specific guidelines for assignment and course completion dates. Please make sure you are aware of the course requirements and due dates.

- **Learn and study without being on campus:** Online learning allows learners to take courses from a distance, saves travelling and commuting times and generally provides more flexibility to students.

- **Accessibility to extra resources**: Learning online releases the power of the Internet and your ability to access the vast resources available through the Internet and other electronic mediums. Some courses include links to other Internet sites that provide relevant and useful information related to your course. Using the Internet you can conduct searches for additional information to help you complete papers and assignments.

- **Participation with a "community" of learners**: WebCT courses provide a variety of communication tools such as a bulletin board, electronic mail (e-mail) and online chat. These tools allow you to regularly communicate with other students in your course.

- **Access and communication with instructors and facilitators:** Students have direct access to instructors and facilitators through the course communication tools.

3.7   Internet Protocols and Etiquette

Protocols and etiquette for using the Internet are constantly changing and evolving - just like the Internet itself!

A few considerations and points to enrich your online learning experience include:

- **Courtesy and Respect:** Courtesy and respect that apply in the ordinary classroom also apply online, and require even more attention.

- **Participate:** In the online environment simply viewing and reading notes isn't enough - that's like showing up for class and never talking to anyone, or simply not showing up and copying someone's notes who did attend class! To gain the most from your learning experience, others need to know your opinions, suggestions, thoughts, beliefs and experiences. Your active participation and comments add to the information, the shared learning, and the sense of community in each course.

- **Enjoy the Technology:** Using the Internet and computers for learning is relatively new. Students completing online courses report learning a lot about the Internet and computers. Don't be intimidated if you experience some problems and challenges. You can seek help from your fellow learners and your instructor.

- **Share Information:** For many, taking an online course is a new experience. By sharing your information, tips and suggestions everyone can benefit from your experience and knowledge.

- **Did You Say What You *Really* Mean?** In everyday face-to-face conversations you have the chance to read a person's non-verbal reactions to what you've said and you can clarify if necessary. For online courses, we rely on the written word only. While you can't anticipate all reactions, do read over what you've written before you send it.

- **You are not alone!** Remember that other people can read what you've written and contributed to the course. Although it is easy to assume that you're working in isolation on your computer, others are also participating!

3.8 Communicating Online

Communicating online - using bulletin board postings, e-mail messages or chat sessions - is substantially different than traditional classroom discussions. A few pointers to keep in mind:

- **Think Before You Click!** Re-read or preview your message before you send it to ensure it says what your *really* mean. Could the receiver take your message another way than you intended it?

- **Overreacting:** Sometimes you may read a message or posting that you disagree with. Constructive debate and confrontation can be very helpful to the learning experience. However, be cautious not to react with too much emotion or anger to a comment. This is considered "flaming" and is inappropriate for online communication. Remember, once you have clicked the send button it is too late!

- **One Subject Only Please!** Focus on one subject per message and always include a pertinent subject title for the message, that way the user can locate the message quickly.

- **Citations:** Cite all quotes, references and sources and respect copyright and license agreements.

- **Format:** The following are some suggestions for formatting your messages:

  ➢ Capitalize words only to highlight an important point or to distinguish a title or heading. Capitalizing whole words that are not titles is generally termed as SHOUTING!

  ➢ *Asterisks* surrounding a word can be used to make a stronger point.

  ➢ Limit line length to approximately 65-70. The course system will do this automatically for you as long as you have "line wrap" activated when composing messages.

  ➢ You may want to add your name to the end of your message as a courtesy.

  ➢ If you are replying to a specific message, you may want to copy portions of the original message in your response. Using the "quote" button to respond to messages and postings in the E-mail system and bulletin board will copy the sender's message with your response.

- **Emotion:** Text messages make it difficult to convey emotion. So, a series of symbols entitled "emoticons" that can be entered from any keyboard and added to messages have been developed to demonstrate the emotion intended in the message. Here are a few commonly used emoticons you may want to use in your messages:

  ➢ :-) Your basic smiley. This smiley is used for a joking statement since we can't hear voice inflection over e-mail.

- ;-) Winky smiley. User just made a sarcastic remark. More of a "don't hit me for what I just said" smiley.

- :-(Frowning smiley. User did not like that last statement or is upset or depressed about something.

- :-I Indifferent smiley.

- :-> A really biting sarcastic remark. Worse than a ;-).

- >:-> A really devilish remark.

Treat 46 or 48